# Sudan, Darfur

## and the

# Nomadic Conflicts

# Sudan, Darfur and the Nomadic Conflicts

Our World Divided

**Philip Steele**

rosen publishing's
rosen
central

New York

# Chapter 1
# Sudan on the brink

**J**uba isn't a big city – yet. In January 2011 this small port on the banks of the White Nile did not have any crowded squares or high-rise buildings. It did not have any fashionable shopping streets, and major roads were not packed with traffic.

However, an unusual landmark could be seen on a street in Juba. A giant clock showed how many days, hours and minutes were left before election day in the country's big referendum (vote). Excitement was running high. Decisions made on that day might change the city, and all of Sudan, completely.

## A "yes" vote or a "no"?

The question on the ballot would be whether Sudan, Africa's largest nation and the tenth biggest in the world by area, should split in two. A vote in favor of secession (breaking away) might make Juba the capital of a new nation, South Sudan.

This referendum was the result of a 2005 peace agreement, which followed decades of civil war between the northern part of Sudan and the south. Were those terrible days finally to be left behind? And would the government in Khartoum, the northern capital, accept the result of the vote?

## The big poll

At last, between January 9 and 15, 2011, the people voted – not just in Juba, but in small villages and towns all over the south. The result was announced a few weeks later – an overwhelming 99 percent of the southern Sudanese population had voted for independence. In some areas more votes were counted than was possible, but even when these ballots were discounted, there was no doubting the overall result. The celebrations began. Crowds waved flags, and people drummed and danced in the tropical heat. The new state would be founded on July 9, 2011, opening a fresh chapter in African politics.

▲ *Southerners celebrate the break with North Sudan – but can future conflict be avoided?*

# What does the future hold?

Hopes were high, but some people feared that they were too high. South Sudan would, in the future, have revenue from its oil reserves, but as yet it had very little infrastructure such as highways, bridges or even a safe, clean water supply. How would South Sudan cope with refugees returning from the north? Many people had fled north to escape the fighting in the south. Now these people were keen to return and reclaim their land. The years of civil war had taken a severe toll on health, education and development. How could it be possible to start a new nation from scratch? The northerners, a far greater number than the southerners, did not vote in the referendum because it was the south that was considering secession. They did, however, accept the referendum result.

## Peoples and conflict

The different peoples making up Sudan have a long history of ethnic conflict. This has not just been between north and south, but between the various peoples living within these regions. For example, the region of Darfur, in the west of North Sudan, has seen violence since 2003, with villages destroyed and refugees fleeing the area.

This book will look at conflict in Sudan, and try to find out why it has happened. Is it due to history, religion or culture, or is it all about political power or economics? Is it the result of different peoples competing for the same land, water and resources? Is it due to the actions taken by other nations? We will look at how Sudan relates to other countries and consider its record on human rights. We'll look at ways of resolving conflict and consider how things may turn out for Sudan in the future. The result of the 2011 referendum will be important not just for Juba and the new South Sudan, but for the north, for all of Africa and for the rest of the world.

## Viewpoints

"Unity is better than secession. Secession is like a cancer: if it infects the body, it will damage all the other parts."

Al-Sadiq Babiker, resident of Khartoum, the northern capital, as reported by UNIfeed in January 2011

"The results of the referendum mean I am free today... Now I am a first-class citizen in my own country."

Abiong Nyok, housewife and resident of Juba, the southern capital, as reported by the BBC in February 2011

• Almost all southerners supported secession. Most northerners would have voted no – if they had been given the choice.

• What are behind these differences? Might the reasons for disagreement lead to further conflict in the future?

# Chapter 2

# Lands on the Nile

**D**uring the Middle Ages all the lands south of the Sahara Desert, from west to east, were referred to in Arabic as *Bilad al-Sudan*. Later, the term "Sudan" began to be used just for those lands lying between Egypt and Central Africa.

Throughout history Sudan has lain between three distinct cultural zones – Arabia (just across the Red Sea), North Africa and Africa south of the Sahara. The various peoples of these zones have mingled, and clashed, over the ages.

## Ancient Sudan

Sudan has a long history of trade, invasion and migration by nomadic peoples since ancient times. From about 2600 BCE the northernmost region of Sudan, known as Cush, traded with ancient Egypt. Eventually the Egyptians invaded and came to rule all of Cush.

▲ *Sudan is crossed by the White Nile and Blue Nile rivers, which join together at the northern cities of Khartoum and Omdurman. The country includes hot sandy deserts, mountains and wide plains. In the south, there is a vast watery wilderness known as the Sudd.*

**KEY**

- NORTH SUDAN
- SOUTH SUDAN
- ABYEI PROVINCE

# Arabs and Islam

In the 500s CE Christianity reached northern Sudan from Egypt and Ethiopia. It was followed by Islam after the Arabs conquered Egypt in 642 CE and traveled into Sudan. Over the next 900 years, Arab nomads and traders moved into northern and central Sudan. They married into local African communities. Their descendants identified with Islam and the Arab way of life, and they enjoyed the wealth brought from trade. However, the Arabs did not settle in the south, with its tropical climate and swamps. The south had been home to cattle herders for thousands of years, with movements of tribes into and across the region continuing into the 1500s CE.

# Invaders and slavers

In 1805 Muhammad Ali, a commander in the Ottoman (Turkish) army, won control of Egypt. From 1820 to 1823 his troops invaded northern Sudan. From there they launched violent attacks on the south, killing many local people and capturing slaves. The horrors of this slave trade left lasting bitterness between the north and south of Sudan, and still divides the country today.

Muhammad Ali died in 1849. Egypt faced big economic problems, and its government became weak. Britain and France grew more powerful in Egypt, and they also wanted to control Sudan. Sudan bordered the Red Sea, near the new Suez Canal, which was vital for international trade to pass from the Red Sea across Sudan, into British and French colonies in East and Central Africa. Explorers were also mapping the course of the Nile River at this time. It was a great resource for the whole region, and both Britain and France wanted control of it. Britain became the biggest power in Egypt and, in 1877, the Egyptian government appointed a famous British soldier, Charles Gordon, as Governor-General of all Sudan.

▲ *Governor-General Charles Gordon was killed in Khartoum in 1885. His statue (above) was removed from Sudan after independence in 1956.*

## Sudan rises up

From 1881 to 1885, Sudan was swept by a mass uprising against Egyptian rule and its British representatives. This was led by Muhammad Ahmad, an Islamic leader known as the Mahdi (meaning "Divine Guide"). His followers besieged and captured the capital, Khartoum, in 1885. A British relief force arrived too late to save Gordon, and he was killed. The Mahdi died that same year, but the independent Islamic state he created, known as the Mahdiya, survived for over a decade.

## Revenge at Omdurman

Then, in 1898, the British army invaded northern Sudan. They defeated the Mahdiya army near Omdurman (see map, page 8). Some 9,700 Sudanese were killed. The British troops were armed with deadly machine guns and artillery, but they were astonished by the fierce resistance put up by the Sudanese, who fought with simple spears and rifles.

## Empire building

The British then started reconquering the rest of Sudan. In the process they quarreled with France. The British

# Case Study

## The "Mahdi"

The best known landmark in the city of Omdurman today is a shining dome, marking the tomb of Muhammad Ahmad bin Abdallah (the "Mahdi," 1844–85). The original

building was destroyed by the British in 1898, but was rebuilt by Muhammad Ahmad's son in 1947. A North Sudanese Arab, Muhammad Ahmad was an Islamic scholar and mystic who claimed to be descended from the family of the prophet Muhammad. Muhammad Ahmad's teachings were rejected by many Muslims in Sudan, but he won support and loyalty among many northern and western Sudanese, and all those who wanted to end rule from Egypt. The Mahdi believed he had a divine mission to free Sudan, but he died of typhus or perhaps smallpox soon after the uprising. However, the Mahdi revolt permanently affected and shaped the history of northern Sudan.

◄ *The Mahdi was a religious leader who led the opposition to foreign rule.*

wanted Sudan to join up with its new East African territories, while the French wanted to join it with their colonies in West and Central Africa. There was a standoff between military forces of the two nations in southern Sudan, but the French eventually withdrew. These were the years known as the "scramble for Africa," when European nations competed to control the whole African continent.

## Colonial rule

Although Egypt was still technically an independent nation, it had been controlled by Britain since the 1880s. In 1899 Britain and Egypt formally created a new "Anglo-Egyptian" state, which gave Britain lasting power in both Egypt and Sudan. This meant that, until Sudan gained independence in 1956, it was effectively governed as a colony. The Darfur region (see map, page 8) was added to the colonial map after it was invaded by British

and French forces in 1916–17, during World War I (1914–1918).

The British developed the economics of the north of Sudan, introducing cash crops, such as cotton. However, Darfur and the south were largely ignored and denied development. Traditional rivalries between the peoples of the north and south were left unresolved. Religious differences were sharpened, too, with the work of Christian missionaries in the south resented by Muslims in the north.

▲ *Cotton became the chief cash crop in northern Sudan from 1925.*

# Conflict in Sudan: key events

**1956** Sudan gains independence as a single nation, as fighting breaks out between north and south.

**1955-72** The first Sudanese civil war.

**1978** Discovery of oil in southern Sudan.

**1983-2005** The second Sudanese civil war.

**2003** Start of antigovernment rebellion in Darfur.

**2004** Bombing of Darfur by government and attacks on civilians by Janjawid militias.

**2011** South Sudan votes to break away from the north.

## Independent Sudan

From 1923 some Sudanese began to campaign for an end to British rule. Rebel military officers founded a nationalist movement called the White Flag League. By 1953 the age of empire was ending, and the British were prepared to discuss self-government. Sudan's independence from British rule was declared in 1956. Even before then, fighting had broken out among the Sudanese peoples. Southerners had demanded a handing over of some power to the south, or even full secession. There were economic problems, too, caused by the low price of cotton on world markets. In 1955 the Sudanese military seized power in Sudan, and a full-scale civil war began in the south, led by a movement called Anyanya.

## Troubled times

The 1960s saw strikes, economic crises, a return to civilian rule and finally, in 1969, another military coup, led by Colonel Jaafar an-Nimeiry. The first civil war ended in 1972, when a peace deal agreed upon in Ethiopia offered greater powers to the south. Then, in 1983, Nimeiry imposed a strict version of the Islamic law, known as Shari'a, across all of Sudan. This enraged many people of the south, where most people followed either traditional African beliefs or the Christian faith.

In 1983 the civil war between north and south flared up again. Southerners rearmed under the Sudan People's Liberation Movement (SPLM).

▲ *Prime Minister Ismail al-Azhari (center) proclaims an independent Sudan in 1956.*

Oil had been discovered in the south in 1978, and now oil installations came under attack from southern rebels who did not want the oil revenue from these installations benefitting northern Sudan.

In 1985 Nimeiry was overthrown by the Sudanese military. Hard times lay ahead, with war and famine in neighboring countries. Refugees poured into eastern Sudan from Ethiopia, and into Darfur from Chad. In 1989 there was another military coup, bringing to power General Omar al-Bashir. The north-south civil war dragged on. Bombing of the south led many refugees to flee across the border into Uganda.

## Terrorists and tension

In the 1990s, the US was becoming increasingly concerned about the policies of the Bashir government in Khartoum. Iran, which had opposed the US since 1979, had declared support for the north and supplied Bashir's government

▲ *Anyanya fighters battle for southern secession in 1971.*

forces with aircraft and tanks. A wealthy Saudi Arabian named Osama bin Laden settled in Sudan and tried to develop it as a base for a terrorist organization called al-Qaeda. He was expelled to Afghanistan in 1996 (from which, five years later, he would organize the 9/11 terrorist attacks against the US). He was killed by US forces in Pakistan in May 2011.

Tensions between the US and Sudan continued to build. The US imposed sanctions against Sudan on the grounds of support for terrorism and human rights abuses. In 1998 there was a US missile attack on the al-Shifa pharmaceutical plant in the Khartoum North region. The US government claimed that this factory was the site of a chemical weapons program, linked with al-Qaeda. The attack was seen by many as revenge for terrorist attacks carried out on US embassies in Africa. Critics in and outside Sudan strongly denied the accusations and disputed evidence regarding chemical weapons.

Zaghawa ethnic groups fled across the border into Chad.

## Rebellion in Darfur

In 2003 a rebellion by opponents of Bashir's government broke out in Darfur, in the western part of the country. Antigovernment forces calling themselves the Sudan Liberation Movement (SLM) accused the Sudan government of discriminating against local ethnic groups. Khartoum politicians claimed the SLM and other groups were funded, armed and trained by the West, in order to destabilize Sudan and win control of its oil. The SLM later joined forces with the Justice and Equality Movement (JEM), an Islamic group that attacked oil fields in the Abyei province.

## Villages on fire

In 2004 the Khartoum government retaliated and bombed Darfur. Bashir was accused of hiring local militias called the Janjawid to suppress the rebellion. The Janjawid attacked rebels and civilians with great brutality. They burned down villages, raped and murdered. Hundreds of thousands of people were killed or died from disease. Many from the Fur and

## Human rights outcry

There was increasing criticism of Bashir by the West, by the United Nations (UN) and by NGOs (nongovernmental organizations, such as international aid and medical agencies) and by human rights groups. As a result, some of these international groups were expelled from Darfur by Bashir's government.

Peace was eventually reached between the government and the SLM in 2006, but there were many arguments between Khartoum and the West over the use of UN troops as peacekeepers. In 2008 a joint African Union-United Nations force, under UN command, was set up in Darfur. Peace talks between the government and representatives of other rebel factions continued to take place in 2010–11, but conflict still remains.

Human rights activists blamed President Bashir for the Darfur atrocities. In 2009 Bashir was cited by the International Criminal Court (ICC) for war crimes and crimes against humanity. In 2010 the ICC also called for Bashir's arrest for genocide – an attempt to destroy a whole people.

These legal moves were opposed by the African Union and large parts of the international community. Bashir's defenders deny that his government planned the Janjawid attacks in Darfur. They claim that Western condemnation is an attempt to control Sudanese oil and resources.

▲ *Many villages were burned across Darfur, displacing thousands of civilians.*

▲ *Since 2004 more than 260,000 refugees from Darfur have crossed into Chad. More than 85 percent of them are women and children.*

## North-South accord

Meanwhile, in 2005, the second civil war between north and south ended at last. The peace accord, signed in Naivasha, Kenya, in 2005 had paved the way for the referendum on secession in 2011. The successful result was an event many southerners had believed they would never live to see.

The international community was surprised that the result was accepted by Bashir. However, suggestions that, as a reward, the charges against him at the ICC should be dropped were rejected by human rights activists. In 2011 Bashir announced that he will resign before the next election in North Sudan in 2015.

## Fact panel

| | North Sudan | South Sudan |
|---|---|---|
| Name: | Republic of the Sudan | Republic of South Sudan |
| Capital: | Khartoum | Juba |
| Language: | Mainly Arabic | Mainly English |
| Major towns: | Khartoum North, Omdurman, Port Sudan | Malakal, Bor, Wau, Bentiu, Torit, Kapoeta |
| Main religions: | Mostly Islam, some Christianity | Traditional African beliefs, Christianity, some Islam |
| Resources: | Natural gas, oil | Oil, timber |

## All of Sudan

Area: 2,505,813 sq km (967,450 sq miles). Until the border is settled, final figures cannot be confirmed for the separate nations.

Population: More than 45 million. Estimates for the southern population alone vary from 8 million to 13 million.

# Chapter 3

# Peoples divided?

**N**orth and South Sudan are diverse lands. There are believed to be 132 different languages across the whole region, spoken by 56 major ethnic groups – and these may be divided into as many as 600 subgroups. Furthermore, many of these groups have been scattered and fragmented by years of conflict and by the migration of refugees.

Many people speak several languages. Arabic is the common language in the north, while English is understood by many in the south. The linguistic divide between north and south has encouraged a sense of difference between northerners and southerners. Might Sudan's regional conflicts and the secession of the south have a basis in a lack of national identity?

## Viewpoints

"Polarization [division into two contrasting groups]... has afflicted the country [Sudan] with a crisis of national identity."

"Only through mutual recognition, respect and harmonious interaction among African and Arab populations...can Sudan ensure a just and lasting peace."

Two quotes from the book *War of Visions*, 1995, by Francis M. Deng, diplomat, academic and, from 2007 to 2012, Special Advisor on the Prevention of Genocide at the United Nations.

• The many layers of Sudanese identity have become inflamed by decades of civil war. Will they be healed or made worse by the secession of the south?

## Living in the north

Life in North Sudan is very different from life in South Sudan. The climate is very hot and dry, and there are large areas of desert.

▲ *This satellite image of Sudan shows the vast difference between the hot, dry landscape of the north and the tropical vegetation of the south.*

▲ *Northern men in the small town of Kerma wear white robes and turbans.*

Northerners may work in factories, on farms or as market traders. More people in the north are city dwellers. There are also nomadic peoples in the north, living by herding camels, goats or cattle. Northern buildings may be made of concrete or of traditional mud brick, with flat roofs.

Northern dress is generally Arab in style, with men often wearing the loose cotton robe, or *jalabiya*, and a white turban or a white skullcap. Women wear full-length gowns with a cotton scarf draped over the head and shoulders. The cloth is often colorful, although in the northeast it is more likely to be black. Northern food is very like that eaten in Egypt – dishes of beans known as *fuul*, bread, lentils, lamb or goat. Tea and coffee are offered to guests.

Most northerners follow the Sunni branch of the Islamic faith. Islamic law, known as Shari'a, introduced by Nimeiry in 1983, has been a major political issue affecting aspects of life, such as what clothing can be worn and harsh punishments for crimes.

## Northern perspectives

Northerners are made up of many separate ethnic groups, including Nubians, Arabs, Beja, Fur and Baggara. Many northerners see themselves as very distinct from the Egyptians to the north, and as superior to the peoples of the south. However the reality is that many of them share the same African ancestry as the southerners.

"Slave" is still a harsh term of abuse sometimes directed toward southerners, even though many northerners are themselves descended from slaves. Traditional customs followed by many southern peoples, such as the wearing of clothes that show more flesh, are condemned by many northerners as un-Islamic. Many people in South Sudan do not follow Islam. Their religions and beliefs have different teachings about traditional dress.

## The southern way of life

Young people growing up in South Sudan experience a very different way of life. This region has a hot, humid, tropical climate with heavy seasonal rains. There are few big cities and farming is more likely to be at a subsistence level, supplying food for the family and community rather than cash crops for export. Many people are cattle herders or Nile fishermen. Their staple food is a porridge made from millet. Southern villages are generally made up of round huts with thatched roofs, surrounded by thorn hedges to pen the livestock. Most southern men wear T-shirts, shorts or trousers, while women wear cotton dresses or skirts. In some regions people wear little clothing or leather kilts and beads. Southern ethnic groups include the Dinka, Nuer, Shilluk and Azande.

## Refugees and religion

The years of civil war scattered southern communities in all directions. To escape the violence, some refugees fled abroad and eventually sought asylum in Western countries. Many fled north to cities unaffected by the war, where most suffered from poverty. Some were forcibly taken from the south to the north and were forced to work for nothing or were sexually exploited. Many of these people lived poverty-stricken and exploited lives, experiencing virtual slavery in the north. About four million refugees returned home to South Sudan for the secession.

Some southern Sudanese Christians resent Islamization and feel they have been persecuted by the north. For others, religion is not the chief issue. Often religion is the way in which a conflict finds its expression. The real causes may be very different, such as political oppression or poverty.

## Ethnic divisions

The north-south divide owes a lot to history. Over the centuries northerners raided the south to seize slaves, and the long years of civil war have done little to ease tensions between the people of Sudan. To what extent is it due to ethnicity? Are ethnic divisions at the heart of Sudan's conflicts? They certainly played a part in the Sudanese civil wars and the Darfur conflict.

▲ *A southern Sudanese family starts the day, cooking and eating outside their home.*

# Root causes of conflict

There has always been conflict between ethnic groups in Africa, as elsewhere in the world. In Sudan there has been war, violence, enslavement and discrimination. Aggression based upon ethnic identity and racism has certainly played a part in this. However, the differences between two ethnic groups are often much less than people believe. Conflict is often based on other, deeper causes that go beyond ethnicity.

The reasons may be economic. One ethnic group might be poor, with no access to resources, while another may own sources of wealth. In southern Sudan, cattle herders may compete for the best pasture, or steal livestock from another community. This has long been a cause of trouble between the Nuer and the Dinka peoples, for example, two of the largest ethnic groups in South Sudan.

▶ *Tensions between ethnic groups mean this Dinka fighter keeps his weapon close while he guards his community.*

# Viewpoints

"...For us here there is no government."

A man from the Nuba community of South Kordofan, quoted in a report by the US-based National Democratic Institute, March 2009

"An estimated 250 people in central Sudan have been killed during a week of clashes between nomadic groups."

BBC News, May 29, 2009

• Nomadic groups often fight over the water they need for their cattle. In May 2009 about 250 fighters were killed in South Kordofan during clashes over grazing land.

• Are land disputes aggravated by other problems? Political rivalries, lawlessness, poverty and the return of refugees to claim their land have all played their part in the conflicts.

## Competing for land

Conflict occurs when political systems do not consider the different needs of nomadic and settled peoples. In the west, on the edge of the Sahara, nomads struggle to survive in regions that seem to become drier each year. Nomadic peoples, in search of pasture or water, sometimes raid or invade the lands that are permanently settled by farming and fishing communities.

## The legacy of colonization

Current violence between ethnic groups in Africa is often rooted in the politics of the last two centuries. During the 1800s when the European empire builders drew up the borders of their new African colonies (see page 9), they were often less concerned with the peoples they ruled than with their own political rivalries, or with resources and trade. Borders of territories often passed straight through historical homelands, dividing peoples and cultures.

Ethnic conflict was sometimes used to prevent a united opposition arising, a policy referred to as "divide and rule". European rulers in Africa might recruit the army from one ethnic group, for example, and the civil service, such as the government administration, from another. In Sudan little was done to bring peoples together, to improve economic conditions or provide education and security.

## Effects of warfare

In the past, violent differences that broke out between ethnic groups could sometimes be resolved by traditional leaders, who might negotiate peace or, for example, agree on compensation for stolen cattle. However during the long years of civil war, traditional social structures and safeguards broke down among the peoples of the south. Automatic weapons replaced custom and negotiation.

## Current dangers

There have already been outbreaks of violence since the vote for South Sudanese succession was declared in Febuary 2011. The two new nations remain very closely linked, both geographically and by the economics of oil. Oil production and distribution relies on close cooperation between North and South Sudan. People fear that the new peace will be threatened if there is political disagreement over oil and the division of profits.

The border regions between North and South Sudan could make or break the success of secession, particularly in oil-rich Abyei. The referendum on secession in Abyei has not taken place, due to disputes over terms. It is the home of the Dinka Ngok people, who align with the south. However the Misseriya nomads, who pass through the region with their herds, align with the north. Tensions

▲ *Life is tough for nomads in the harsh desert lands of North Sudan.*

# Case Study

*For traditional Dinka communities, cattle are all-important.*

## When there were no more cattle

During the civil war, military attacks on southern towns and villages by government forces scattered whole families. Those who escaped the fighting risked their lives fleeing the country. Peoples such as the Dinka did not only lose lives, land and power – they lost their cattle. In traditional Dinka communities, cattle are more than livestock. They are a currency, used to pay dowries for brides. They are a part of Dinka myth, legend and culture, and a source of great pride. The loss of cattle meant a loss of status to a whole ethnic group.

rose further in May 2011, when troops from North Sudan invaded Abyei town. Any more conflict there could start a new war between North and South.

## Continuing conflict

There are further ethnic conflicts simmering within South Sudan, where rebel groups known as the Southern Sudan Democratic Movement have set themselves against South Sudan's government. People from the Nuer ethnic group complain that the Dinka will have too much influence in the new administration. And within the boundaries of North Sudan lies Darfur, where a formal peace agreement has not yet been reached.

# Chapter 4

# Politics and power

There have been great changes in Sudan since the establishment of South Sudan as an independent nation. However, it has not meant a sudden break with the past.

After the peace agreement was reached in 2005, Sudan adopted an interim constitution. A constitution is the legal framework by which any nation is governed. In accordance with this, Sudan had a Government of National Unity (GNU), which allowed for powers to be shared with a South Sudanese Legislative Assembly. This meant that it was already possible to form an administration-in-waiting in Juba before the 2011 referendum.

## Voting in 2010

The last parliamentary and presidential elections to be held in a united Sudan took place in April 2010. There were many flaws in the process and accusations of vote rigging. However, the result was accepted and confirmed Omar al-Bashir as president and his National Congress Party (NCP) as the winners. It also confirmed Salva Kiir as the southern president-to-be and the SPLM as the leading political party in the South. The SPLM must now prove itself as a national government. It offers a democratic program.

▲ *Southern leader Salva Kiir (left) meets with controversial northern president Omar al-Bashir.*

# Case Study

## Bashir and Kiir — two leaders, two nations

It seems likely that the fate of the two Sudans will, for the time being, be steered by two very different people. Omar al-Bashir was born to the north of Khartoum in 1944, in the days before independence. He was a successful military commander before seizing power in 1993. Bashir has always been a controversial leader, and as a result of the atrocities in Darfur, he became the first serving head of state in the world to be charged with genocide before the International Criminal Court.

While Bashir often wears traditional Arab dress, Salva Kiir, the southern president, is known for wearing a broad-brimmed cowboy style hat. He was born into the Dinka ethnic group in 1951 and is a veteran of both Sudanese civil wars, fighting with Anyanya and then the SPLA, a military wing of the SPLM (see page 12). He has a very large political following in South Sudan, and he has promised a democratic future.

The two men have worked together already: following the interim constitution of 2005, Kiir was vice president to Bashir's president.

## The Darfur factor

Although al-Bashir originally came to power in a military coup, his NCP is now a democratic party. However it has been repeatedly criticized by Western governments for abuses of human rights. Its harsh rule was shown at its most extreme at the height of the Darfur crisis, which resulted in so many deaths and so much human misery.

In 2011 al-Bashir announced that he would not be running for reelection in 2015. His indictment for genocide in Darfur by the International Criminal Court remains a thorny issue. It leaves a question mark over the future of government in North Sudan, both before and after Bashir's planned departure.

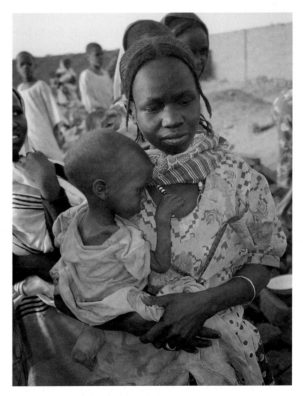

▲ *A mother holds her malnourished child in North Darfur. The atrocities of Darfur were brought to the world's attention through the media.*

## Sudan and the world

International politics will play an important part in the future of both North and South Sudan. The relations between the northern government and the Western powers, especially the US, have been difficult for many years. However, relations with China are close, both in North and South Sudan, due to economic cooperation (see page 30). China is the world's second biggest economic power and the world's fastest growing economy.

## Neighbors and change

Neighboring nations are also crucial to the future of both nations. South Sudan is already closely linked to Uganda and its neighbors in Central Africa. Juba is much nearer to Kampala, the Ugandan capital, than it is to Khartoum, the capital of North Sudan. Drought, famine, war or political unrest in Chad or Ethiopia could, at any time, bring a new flood of refugees across Sudan's borders, straining natural resources and creating even more competition for food and land use.

A new wind is blowing from countries in the north and east as well. Shortly after Sudan's referendum in 2011, an extraordinary series of protests and revolts broke out across the Arab world, as people demanded political freedom or reform. The outcome of these is as yet unknown, but they will affect North Sudan especially. Egypt's President Hosni Mubarak (who had opposed South Sudan's secession) was overthrown in February 2011. In October 2011 Libya's President Muammar Gaddafi was overthrown and killed. Protests also took place in Khartoum, perhaps a sign of future challenges facing the government in North Sudan.

# Viewpoints

"[The United Nations Development Program (UNDP) is] empowering people across Sudan to achieve sustainable peace and development. All our development efforts support the implementation of the peace agreements across the country. Whether in Khartoum, Juba, El-Fasher or Kassala, our strategic interventions aim to develop the capacity of institutions, civil society, and communities to help them consolidate peace, prevent more conflicts, and build a better life."

UNDP Sudan mission statement

"Omar al-Bashir, the Sudanese president, has warned the United Nations mission in Darfur and foreign aid organizations to 'support government authorities' or face expulsion."

Al Jazeera news, August 2010

• Since the 1970s the United Nations, the world's largest international treaty organization, has condemned Sudan for human rights abuses and sponsoring terrorism.

• The UN is not always popular with some Sudanese, a view shared in other parts of Africa. Its critics believe that the UN's most powerful body, the Security Council, is unfairly dominated by Western powers and claims that they are as interested in political control and resources as they were during the age of empires.

• However, the UN remains a crucial organization to help both north and south move forward, and it is already involved in peacekeeping and in a variety of aid projects in Sudan.

▲ *US President Barack Obama addresses the UN General Assembly about the future of Sudan in September 2010.*

# Chapter 5
# Water, oil and land

**M**uch of the conflict between the peoples of Sudan, and between Sudan and the rest of the world, is about economics. Sudan is still a very poor region of the world, although the economy is rapidly being transformed by oil.

In 2010, as a single nation, the value of the goods and services produced in Sudan per person (what economists call the gross domestic product, or GDP, per capita) was ranked 140th out of 183 nations in the world. Thanks to oil production, Sudan's GDP in 2010 increased by more than 5 percent. Yet average life expectancy in Sudan was still only 54 years, and 40 percent of the population lived below the poverty line.

## North vs. South

In 2010, only 7 percent of the workforce, north and south, were employed in the manufacturing industry, and only 13 percent in service industries. Eighty percent worked on the land, herding (camels, goats, and sheep in the north; cattle in the south), fishing or growing crops.

The north has always had the largest towns and the biggest workforce. It is where most Sudanese factories are located, and so it has an economic advantage over the south.

South Sudan, undeveloped and ravaged by war, faces huge problems. It needs roads, schools and health care.

## Troubled waterways

Sudan's oldest and greatest natural resource is its river. The Nile is not a single waterway, but a maze of tributaries and swamps feeding into the Blue Nile and White Nile, which merge at Khartoum. The river has always been vital for human use, for livestock, for growing crops and for transportation.

The Nile gives Sudan great strategic importance, as Sudan's use of the river also affects the lives of people in Uganda, Kenya, Rwanda, Burundi, the Democratic Republic of the Congo, Tanzania and Ethiopia. Downstream, the whole economy of Egypt depends utterly on the water from Sudan. In the past Egypt has even threatened war over the river, so the Nile could be a cause of future conflict, perhaps the major cause.

The river nations negotiate with each other through a forum called the Nile Basin Initiative. In 2010 the five upstream nations of Rwanda, Kenya, Ethiopia, Uganda and Tanzania, who believe that Egypt's share of use is excessive and unjust, reached an agreement among themselves to take more water from the Nile. This caused concern in Egypt and in Sudan. A new agreement will be vital to the future of both North and South Sudan.

◀ *Southern villagers use a dugout canoe to catch fish in the White Nile. The fish may be preserved by drying on racks at riverside fishing camps.*

27

There will also need to be agreement on the proposed construction of the Jonglei Canal in South Sudan. This vast project, delayed by the civil war, involves altering the course of the White Nile to bypass the swamps of the Sudd (see map, page 8). South Sudan fears that the current agreement would increase the amount of water reaching North Sudan and Egypt but would dry out large areas of South Sudan, causing social, economic and environmental problems.

# Oil – blessing or curse?

Wherever oil is found, it brings wealth and development – but it may also bring outside political interference, corporate greed, environmental damage and, sometimes, war.

Oil and natural gas exploration took place across Sudan in the 1970s, led by the US-based Chevron Corporation. In the north, gas was discovered offshore in the Red Sea in 1976. Oil was first discovered in southern Sudan at Bentiu, in 1978. In 1990 Chevron pulled out of Sudan because of the civil war and interests passed to various other companies and to the Khartoum government. Today the biggest operator in Sudan is China's National Petroleum Corporation. Oil has given a great boost to the Sudanese economy, although government corruption has meant this has been of little benefit to the poor and displaced. It is estimated that by 2014, production will reach 8.4 million barrels a day. However, oil reserves may only last about 30 years, so planning for the longer term is vital. That means spending the oil revenue on developing agriculture, industry and education across Sudan.

▲ *China has invested billions of dollars in Sudanese oil and 60 percent of Sudan's oil exports go to China.*

# Viewpoints

"In our case, there is a forced economic cooperation [between north and south], if not a desired one...both parties need to cooperate economically to make things go smoothly."

Abda el-Mahdi, northerner, former Sudanese State Minister of Finance. Reported by Reuters, January 2011

"SUDAN ARMS BUILDUP HEIGHTENS OIL WAR FEARS"

Headline, United Press International online, April 2011

• Consider the viewpoints above. The choice for both Sudans is cooperation, peace and a chance for a better life, or more war, chaos and poverty. How might this be achieved?

## Who profits from oil?

Most of the oil is either in South Sudan or in the disputed border region of South Kordofan, such as Abyei province. While North Sudan has the necessary pipelines, refineries and access to the Red Sea to export it, South Sudan produces most of the crude oil. The plan is that in the future, the money made by oil production will be split 50-50 between north and south. However there is still a lot of mistrust about the actual figures. Honesty and openness will be needed in the future if conflict is to be avoided.

The two governments, the international community and the oil companies must ensure that any new agreement is fair. Oil revenue should chiefly benefit the people and infrastructure of both Sudans, rather than rich international corporations or corrupt leaders. If this works out, oil revenues could transform the southern economy as well as the northern. If it does not, then it could mean a return to civil war, which would be disastrous to all sides.

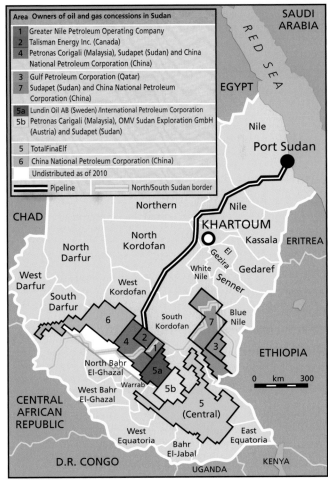

| Area | Owners of oil and gas concessions in Sudan |
|------|--------------------------------------------|
| 1 | Greater Nile Petroleum Operating Company |
| 2 | Talisman Energy Inc. (Canada) |
| 4 | Petronas Corigali (Malaysia), Sudapet (Sudan) and China National Petroleum Corporation (China) |
| 3 | Gulf Petroleum Corporation (Qatar) |
| 7 | Sudapet (Sudan) and China National Petroleum Corporation (China) |
| 5a | Lundin Oil AB (Sweden) /International Petroleum Corporation |
| 5b | Petronas Carigali (Malaysia), OMV Sudan Exploration GmbH (Austria) and Sudapet (Sudan) |
| 5 | TotalFinaElf |
| 6 | China National Petroleum Corporation (China) |
| | Undistributed as of 2010 |
| ▬▬▬ Pipeline | ▭▭▭ North/South Sudan border |

▲ *This map shows the spread of oil and gas installations across North and South Sudan.*

## The Chinese connection

The People's Republic of China is not just Sudan's major oil developer and the biggest importer of Sudanese oil. It is Sudan's biggest trading partner. China is heavily involved in Sudan's finances, in building roads, dams and bridges and in agricultural production across North Sudan. In 2011, it signed a $1.2 billion contract with North Sudan for a new Khartoum airport.

China is building close relations with South Sudan, too, based on shared oil interests, and it has plans to develop the infrastructure there. Plans are being considered to build a pipeline southeast to the Kenyan coast to give South Sudan a pipeline for export that is not dependent on North Sudan. The costs of such a project would be huge.

## Foreign business

Is China's involvement in Sudan a new form of imperialism or empire building? Over 58 percent of Sudan's exports go to China, while 22 percent of imports into Sudan come from China. Why is this welcomed by the Sudanese when the old imperial powers, such as Britain, are not? This may be because China does not interfere in the political affairs of African nations in the way that Western nations have done. However, some in the West claim economy and politics can never really be separated.

Other countries are also heavily involved in Sudanese agriculture, notably Saudi Arabia, a nearby desert country with a great need for access to food crops. Across Africa there is talk of

# Case Study

## Construction and protest: the dam

Development, despite its benefits, will often be the cause of yet more conflict if it is pushed

a "land grab" (an aggressive taking of land) by foreign investors and concern that foreign interests do not benefit local Sudanese needs.

through against the wishes of local Sudanese people.

In March 2009 an enormous new dam was completed at Hamdab, to the north of Merowe in North Sudan.

It harnesses the powers of the Nile River for generating electricity. The dam was the biggest hydroelectric construction project in Africa. The chief contracting companies were Chinese, German and French. It was financed with Chinese, Arab and Sudanese government money. Is this a good example of developing the infrastructure of North Sudan? Sudan certainly has little electricity, only about 7 percent of that of Egypt.

However, the project was heavily criticized. Questions were asked about the destruction of Nubian archaeological sites and the potential damage to the wider environment. Tens of thousands of people were forced to leave their homes and be resettled, and there was very little consultation. Farmers complained that they were deprived of their local water supplies.

◄ *Water, power and politics: the Merowe Dam straddles the Nile.*

Economics is at the center of conflict in Sudan. Unless development is combined with social justice and equality of opportunity, it could cause further conflict. Responsibility lies with the future governments of both Sudans.

# Chapter 6

# Human rights

What do we mean by "human rights"? They are the basic conditions that we all need in order to lead a decent life, free of injustice, cruelty, violence, slavery or exploitation. Abuses of human rights have been central to Sudan's problems for many years. They must be addressed in order to resolve present and future conflict and build a new politics for the region, now that it is made up of two independent nations.

## Universal rights?

The idea of human rights has developed over the ages in many parts of the world, as part of social custom, lawmaking, politics and religion. From the 1600s and 1700s, Europe and later North America became centers of debate about human rights and society. In 1948 the newly formed United Nations drew up a Universal

▲ *Enforcing human rights protects the vulnerable in society.*

Declaration of Human Rights. The term "universal" means that these rights are considered applicable to all cultures and societies everywhere in the world. Regional human rights treaties have been drawn up since, such as the African Charter on Human and Peoples' Rights in 1986.

These universal human rights have often been challenged on the grounds that they do not allow for regional variances in tradition, or that they reflect only Western values. This has been the case, for example, in debates about the kinds of punishments permitted under the harsher versions of Shari'a law, such as lashings. Shari'a was introduced in Sudan in 1983 (see page 17) but now only applies to Muslims in North Sudan. Shari'a law specifies what types of dress are considered appropriate and modest. In northern Sudan, the Public Order Police have harassed women for wearing pants, common items of female clothing in some other Muslim countries.

## Justice and injustice

Another area of debate involves honoring children's rights. In poor countries these rights are often overridden because of economic hardship or the realities of living in a conflict zone, where many children are orphans and just walking to a school is dangerous.

While it is true that definitions and applications must be sensitive to cultural and economic differences around the world, it is also true that governments may try to hide behind this defense when carrying out acts of injustice. No religious or social tradition can justify cruelty, murder or slavery.

Constitutions in Sudan have emphasized a commitment to human rights. The 2005 interim constitution guaranteed religious rights, language and ethnic rights, social justice, children's rights, women's rights and gender equality. Other areas of the constitution were less clear. Clause 16 (i) stated, "*The State shall enact laws to protect society from corruption, delinquency and social evils and steer society as a whole towards virtuous social values consistent with religions and cultures of the Sudan.*"

# Viewpoints

"The Sudanese government should not use violence to cut off peaceful demonstrations and political expression."

Daniel Bekele, Africa director, Human Rights Watch

"The Sudanese people can see that Human Rights Watch is unfair to Sudanese issues in general."

Ibrahim Gandour, National Congress Party, 2010

• Daniel Bekele is the director of an organization campaigning for human rights around the world.

• Ibrahim Gandour is a member of the National Congress Party, the ruling party in North Sudan.

• Consider the motives of the people reporting on Sudan above.

Such clauses can be interpreted in many ways – terms such as "social evil," "delinquency" and "virtuous" are not clearly defined.

## Ideal and reality

Perhaps even more important than the constitution itself is whether human rights really are observed in practice. Sudan's interim constitution failed to protect the citizens of Darfur from the terror of the attacks on civilians by the Janjawid (see page 14). While Bashir stands accused before the ICC of directing these attacks, the Sudanese constitution could still be said to have completely failed to protect its citizens.

The interim constitution has also failed to protect free speech in the north of Sudan. When it comes to press freedom, the international activist group Reporters Without Borders ranks Sudan as 172nd out of 178 nations when it comes to degrees of press freedom.

▲ *Dinka children from Abyei. They may face more violations of their human rights if the future of the region is not agreed upon swiftly.*

In January 2011 plain-clothes police in Khartoum shut down a newspaper called *al-Midan* for reporting on recent student protests that had taken place in Sudan. They arrested 16 people. This was no surprise to the journalists, as security officers were in the habit of visiting the newspaper offices almost daily. Arab human rights organizations had already been criticizing the Sudanese government for censorship over a long period.

Constitutions before 2005 had similarly failed to protect human rights. During the civil war, there were many severe offenses, including the forced recruitment of child soldiers under the official age of 18 by both the SPLM and government forces. Some of the children were as young as six. There was widespread abuse of political prisoners, and human trafficking also took place during the civil war years. Young southerners were abducted for forced labor or sexual exploitation as slaves, bound for North Sudan or overseas. Abduction also took place within southern communities. Laws against human trafficking are now in place. However, will these laws be enforced?

## Women's rights

Women's rights activists are now active in Sudan, north and south, and they have influenced the drafting of new constitutions. While changes have been happening among the more educated and higher social classes, especially in access to employment, the poorest women in Sudanese society still face many problems.

▼ *Human rights activist and politician Graça Machel visits Kebkabiya, North Darfur, in 2007 to talk to refugees there about the future for Sudan.*

## Gay rights

Southern politicians have generally spoken out in favor of honoring human rights. However there are exceptions. Salva Kiir's record on gay rights has been questioned. He is on record as claiming that there is no homosexuality in Sudan and that if there were, it would be opposed. The issue of gay rights has been a matter of fierce debate recently across the border in Uganda, resulting in violence and murder.

## Ways forward

With the secession of South Sudan came a new constitution for this country. This is seen by human rights activists within and outside Sudan as a great opportunity to make further progress in the field of human rights.

Both northern and southern governments will need to take practical action to enforce future human rights legislation. Above all they must make it their priority to eradicate poverty across the region, a goal that seemed impossible until oil wealth began to change Sudanese politics. Poverty is itself a violation of human rights. All humans have a right to work and fair reward for their labor, and a right to a healthy and safe environment. Many other human rights hinge on poverty, for while it continues there can be no fulfilment of the right to food, to education, to social justice or to equality.

▼ *Women's rights are beginning to be recognized in Sudan, and women are playing an increasingly important part in elections, north and south.*

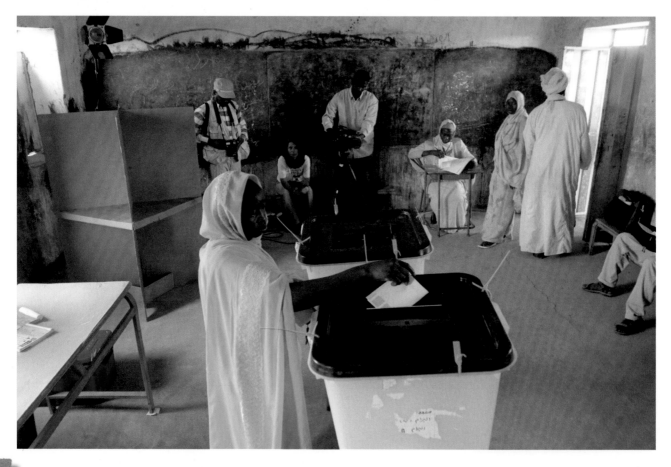

# Case Study

## The right to read

Nine out of ten women in North and South Sudan may be unable to read or write, and nearly four out of ten men. The situation is at its worst in Darfur and in the south. This is the result of poverty and lack of schooling. For generations, education has been interrupted by civil war.

Learning to read and write properly takes most people about five or six years, but in Sudan many children receive less than two years of schooling in total. Literacy allows citizens to improve the way they communicate, to take part in society, to seek employment and to find out about the world. It is regarded by the United Nations not just as a useful skill, but as a basic human right.

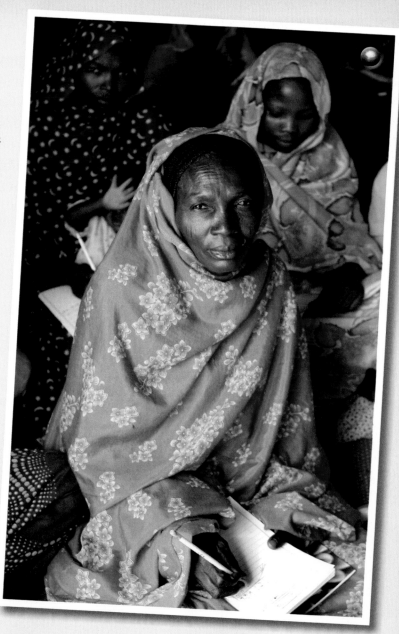

▲ *These refugees from Darfur are learning to write. Literacy is a basic right that will empower Sudanese people and benefit society.*

Many NGOs are working on literacy programs in Sudan. An increase in education is needed to open up opportunities to individuals and benefit both Sudans. Literacy is essential to challenge conflict and poverty in the region.

# Chapter 7

# Hopes and fears

The early months of 2011 saw some developments in northern Sudan every bit as remarkable as the declaration of the secession referendum in Juba. In January, thousands of students and supporters gathered in Khartoum, Omdurman and other northern cities. They protested peacefully against the authoritarian National Congress Party and its president, al-Bashir, demanding an end to government price increases, such as rising food and fuel costs. Security forces and riot police put down the protests in Khartoum with beatings and arrests.

## The "Arab Spring"

These Sudanese protests were inspired by similar events in Egypt and Tunisia, which led to the overthrow of the governments in those countries. During the following months, the Arab and North African cultural zones, which have a great influence on northern Sudan, were in political turmoil. There were protests in Morocco, Algeria, Jordan, Yemen, Bahrain and Syria. Protests against the dictatorship of Muammar Gaddafi in neighboring Libya turned into a full-scale civil war.

The long-term outcome of all these protests remains to be seen, but they do seem to signal a new mood across the region. The response of the Western powers has, say some critics, been inconsistent. Some argue that the West has supported protests against regimes that they disapprove of, as in Libya, but has not intervened against dictators who are its allies. Western nations have continued to sell arms to repressive governments. International relations are always complex, but if the Western powers only call for democracy when they support the likely outcome, it may suggest double standards that weaken their influence.

## After Bashir

Omar al-Bashir's announcement that he will not be running in the next election in 2015 soon followed the protests in 2011. While he said there was no connection with the protests, some said he might be hoping that his statement would diffuse the spreading unrest in northern Sudan. Despite agreeing to resign, the case against him before the International Criminal Court remains unresolved.

So the future for North and South Sudan and all their neighbors suddenly begins to look very different, with a real chance of radical change. However, there will doubtless be setbacks, and reform might be shut down again. The big fear for the future of the new Sudans remains a reignition of conflict – in Darfur, South Kordofan or Abyei. Everything depends on peace and stability for both the new countries to recover and rebuild.

▼ *Riot police attack antigovernment protestors in Khartoum in January 2011. One student died in the protests.*

# Peace at last?

In this book, we have looked at the many sources of conflict between the peoples of Sudan. We have seen that they are not merely down to ethnic or religious differences but are driven forward by historical problems, by economics, by politics, by competition for resources and by injustice and the violation of human rights.

For North Sudan to thrive, peace is needed across Darfur. In the south, secession has offered a great opportunity to start fresh, putting the troubles of the civil war period behind them. For north and south to coexist in peace, many Sudanese agree that the borders of the new states will need to be agreed upon, a fair agreement over oil wealth will need to be reached, and foreign interference should come to an end. They point out that both Sudans and other countries within the region will need to reach a new regional agreement on taking water from the Nile River. Both Sudans must now seek to stop ethnic division and religious intolerance. Their governments will need to invest in education and health care, and universal human rights must be respected.

In such a poor part of the world, every one of these needs will be especially hard to fulfill, and it will not happen overnight. Both Sudans face a long, hard struggle.

# Case Study

## Working for a better future

In southern Sudan, only one in seven children who live past their first birthday survive until their fifth. One reason is the number of infectious, waterborne diseases such as diarrhea and cholera. Only one in fifteen people in the region have access to toilets or washing facilities. Diseases such as

tuberculosis, HIV and AIDS are quite common. Ninety percent of children have not received the vaccinations they need for a healthy life. These figures reveal the health care problems facing the new nation of South Sudan and its government.

United Nations agencies and international charities, such as Oxfam, are working with local people to teach about hygiene, and are training doctors and building schools. Their work is vital, but whether it is sufficient to provide the foundations of a new independent nation is a much-asked question.

▼ *Grasping the future: Villagers discuss hygiene issues at an Oxfam-sponsored workshop in South Sudan.*

## The world watches

For people living in other parts of the world, watching problems unfold in a distant country can leave a feeling of powerlessness and frustration. While governments may take action or the United Nations may step in, what action can individuals take?

First of all, just finding out more about Sudan is a useful, positive step. Find out how people live and what they think. Many Sudanese people come to the West to study – you might invite some of them to talk at your school or college, or take part in a debate.

Follow the news about Sudan in the press or on Internet media sites. Look for contrasting views and opinions about a variety of topics, from economics to politics and from human rights to international aid. Compare the reports for accuracy and bias. Broadcasters and journalists often concentrate on bad news and dramatic disasters – also find out the good news about those in both North and South Sudan who are working to help the people and are determined to build a new future.

▼ *Everyday life continues at the* **souk** *(market) in Omdurman. An end to conflict should help both Sudans prosper.*

# Viewpoints

"It is this that we have waited for, the chance to become an independent country which can grow without oppression from bad leaders."

Voter in the referendum, Juba, 2011

"The root causes of violence will not go away following the referendum."

Alun McDonald, Oxfam East Africa

• The goodwill generated by the 2011 referendum must be matched by a realistic assessment of future problems, if the new Republic of South Sudan is to succeed.

Individuals can offer practical help to North and South Sudan by joining together with others to campaign. Many groups such as Amnesty International campaign for human rights and political prisoners. Other organizations may campaign for women's rights, the welfare of refugees or other causes relevant to the situation in Sudan. Charities may be raising funds for particular projects in Sudan, such as providing clean water or medical care.

In this book we have considered only the case of North and South Sudan. However, many of the issues discussed and many of the political problems are relevant to other countries in Africa, to countries in Asia and in the Americas. Human rights may be at the center of debate in your own country. Conflict resolution is a universal need. In the end, however, the future of both North and South Sudan lies in the hands of the Sudanese people themselves.

▲ *What is the future for this girl in Juba? About 42 percent of the Sudanese population, north and south, are under the age of 14.*

# Timeline

**1820–23** Muhammad Ali, ruler of Egypt, invades northern Sudan. Attacks and slave raids upon the south occur.

**1877** British soldier Charles Gordon is hired by Egypt as Governor-General of all Sudan.

**1881–85** Uprising by the Mahdi. Gordon is killed in Khartoum.

**1898** The Battle of Omdurman. Britain defeats the Islamic state.

**1899** Britain and Egypt jointly rule "Anglo-Egyptian" Sudan.

**1923** Sudanese nationalists begin to oppose British rule. Known as the White Flag League.

**1953** British discuss Sudanese self-government.

**1955** The first Sudanese civil war breaks out.

**1956** Sudanese independence.

**1958** Military coup led by General Ibrahim Abboud.

**1962** Escalation of the war between northern Sudan and southern Sudan, led by Anyanya rebels.

**1964** The October Revolution. Abboud is overthrown, and there is civilian rule.

**1969** Military coup brings Colonel Jaafar an-Nimeiry to power.

**1972** Peace agreement with Anyanya ends first Sudanese civil war.

**1978** Oil is discovered at Bentiu.

**1983** Nimeiry introduces Shari'a law across all of Sudan.

**1983** Start of the second Sudanese civil war under John Garang's SPLA, a military wing of the SPLM.

**1985** Nimeiry is overthrown. There is new military rule until the 1986 election.

**1989** Military coup by the National Salvation Council, chaired by General Omar al-Bashir.

**1992–96** International terrorist Osama bin-Laden is based in Sudan.

**1993** Omar al-Bashir appointed president.

**1998** US missiles target a pharmaceutical plant in Khartoum, claimed to be the site of a chemical weapons program.

**2003** Start of rebellion in Darfur, western Sudan, led by the SLM.

**2004** Khartoum government bombs Darfur. Attacks and atrocities against civilians carried out by Janjawid militias.

**2005** Peace agreement ends second Sudanese civil war.

**2008** United Nations-African Union peacekeeping force established in Darfur.

**2009** Bashir is accused of war crimes by the International Criminal Court.

**2010** Peace talks over Darfur take place, but conflict continues.

**2011** South Sudan votes for secession as an independent nation.

**July 6, 2011** South Sudan separates from North Sudan.

# Glossary

**aid** Financial support, supplies or services offered to a government by the international community.

**accord** An official agreement or treaty.

**atrocity** An act of great cruelty.

**cash crop** A crop grown commercially, for sale or export.

**census** An official count of population and collection of statistical information.

**child soldier** Child forcibly recruited to fight during a war.

**civil war** War between factions within the same nation.

**colonial** Ruled or settled as a colony (a territory governed by another country).

**concession** The right to use land or property for a specific purpose.

**constitution** The framework of laws and principles that determine how a nation is to be governed.

**coup** A sudden seizure of power or overthrow of a government.

**dowry** Property or money that is provided as part of a marriage agreement.

**empire** A group of nations and territories coming under a single ruler or government.

**ethnic group** A group of people sharing the same descent, customs, traditions and often language or religious beliefs.

**gay rights** The civil and sexual rights of homosexual people.

**genocide** The mass murder of a whole people or ethnic group.

**gross domestic product (GDP)** The value of goods and services provided, as an indicator of national wealth.

"GDP per capita" means "GDP per person."

**human rights** The basic needs that must be met if people are to lead a decent life and be treated with justice.

**human trafficking** Trading in human beings for forced labor or sexual exploitation.

**imperial** Having to do with empire.

**imperialism** Building empires to exploit the riches of other lands and peoples.

**indictment** A formal charge or accusation of a serious crime.

**infrastructure** The basic structure and organization needed for modern society to function, such as roads, water supply, sanitation, power and telecommunications.

**interim** For the time being; in the meantime.

**investor** Someone who puts money into a venture in the hope of making a profit.

**Islamization** Applying Muslim laws and customs to a non-Muslim population.

**legislative** Of or concerned with lawmaking.

**militia** A lightly armed force of citizens, separate from an army. It may be either official, semi-official or unofficial.

**nomads** People who are not settled in a permanent home, but who travel from place to place with their herds.

**nongovernmental organization (NGO)** A public or privately run body that operates separately from government.

**referendum** A vote held to decide one particular issue.

**refugee** Someone forced to flee from his or her home by war, hunger, natural disaster or poverty.

**revenue** The money coming in from a certain source, such as oil exports or taxation.

**sanctions** Economic or other measures designed to punish a government for its actions.

**secession** When a region or territory breaks away to form a separate nation.

**secular** Not based on religious values or practices.

**service industries** Industries providing services such as health care, education, insurance, banking, catering or tourism, rather than manufactured goods.

**Shari'a** A code of religious laws and practices acceptable within the Islamic faith, interpreted in various ways.

**staple food** A food that forms the basic part of a diet, such as rice or bread.

**sub-Saharan Africa** The lands lying to the south of the Sahara Desert.

**subsistence farming** Growing crops to feed just a family or community, rather than for wider sale or export.

**terrorism** An attempt to bring about political change by instilling fear in the population, carried out by governments, organizations or individuals.

**universal** Applicable to all people in all situations.

# For More Information

## Books

*Cultures of the World: Sudan* (2nd edition) by Patricia Levy and Zawiah Abdul Latif (Marshall Cavendish Children's Books, 2007)

*Refugee Camp: Surviving the War in Sudan – Carbino's Story* by David Dalton/Médecins Sans Frontières (Ticktock Media, 2006)

## Web Sites

Due to the changing nature of Internet links, Rosen Publishing has developed an online list of Web sites related to the subject of this book. This site is updated regularly. Please use this link to access the list:

http://www.rosenlinks.com/OWD/Sudan

# Index

**Picture Acknowledgments:** The author and publisher would like to thank the following for allowing their pictures to be reproduced in this publication: Marco Di Lauro/Getty Images: Cover; Lynsey Addario/VII Network/Corbis: title page, 14; AFP/Getty Images: 38–39; Mohammed Babiker/XinHua/Xinhua Press/Corbis: 22; Bettmann/Corbis: 12; Jonathan Brady/Alamy: 34; Photo by Father Browne/Universal Images/Getty Images: 9; CPWF Basin Focal Project/flickr: 26–27; Philip Dhil/EPA/Corbis: 6, 30–31; John Downing/Express/Getty Images: 13; Mary Evans Picture Library/Rue des Archives/PVDE: 10; Michael Freeman/Corbis: 21; Robert Harding Picture Library, Ltd./Alamy: 42; The Image Works/Topfoto.co.uk/Photographer FotoWare ColorFactory/Topfoto.co.uk: 19; Marco Di Lauro/Getty Images: 15; Jack Maguire/Alamy: 17; Jenny Matthews/Panos Pictures: 37; Mohamed Messara/EPA/Corbis: 43; The National Archives/HIP/Topfoto.co.uk: 11; Mohamed Nureldin Abdallah/Reuters/Corbis: 35; Oxfam International/Photo by Caroline Gluck/flickr: 40–41; Painet, Inc./Alamy: 18; Ashraf Shazly/AFP/Getty Images: 36; Jason Szenes/EPA/Corbis: 25; Sven Torfin/Panos Pictures: 28; istockphoto: 32; Harvard Art Museum/Fogg Museum, Historical Photographs and special visual collections department, Fine Arts Library: 9; Nikswieweg: 20